FROM THE HEART

Thoughts selected by Beryl Wakefield from

the sermons of

Rev Dr Gordon S. Wakefield

To our family, with love

Introduction

This small book of thoughts is intended for the reader to dip into at random in odd moments, in the hope that the words may spark off reflections and perhaps encourage faith. Perhaps it could be in a handy pocket for those moments spent in the dentist's waiting-room or on the station platform. No attempt has been made to categorise the extracts, so that each must stand on its own.

Gordon began to write sermons and to preach from his earliest years and never doubted his calling. Although he longed to express his love of "the deepest things" in poetry, this was not his metier. So his spiritual and lyrical aspirations emerged in tandem as sermons. They came from one who acknowledged that the study- desk is but a step from the prayer-desk. They also sprang from a deep love of God and many human friendships transcending denominations and backgrounds –a Northumbrian miner, an England cricket captain, an Anglican Archbishop, a Jesuit priest, scholars, poets and musicians. For the last twelve years he was privileged to be asked to write the monthly sermon for the Methodist Recorder, and some of these appeared again in 'Medicines for the Heart' and 'My Providential Way', through the good offices of Church in the Market Place Publications.

It is a perilous enterprise for anyone to select "nuggets" from a life's work, to choose what is deemed to be the essence of thoughts in a concise format. Since Gordon's death I have read several hundreds of his sermons and dare, in love, to believe I can trace the threads. Perhaps they are not always what he would have selected himself! There are themes to which he constantly returned over the long years: the centrality of the Eucharist, the use of imaginative meditation, the Christian life in a cruel world.

Preaching must always be 'from the heart' however strong the intellectual content, its whole raison d'etre is to touch the hearts of the listener or reader with the mystery of the love of God. Gordon was very sensitive to national and world affairs, and often referred to 'this terrible twentieth century'; also to modern scholarship and the new light shed on the Bible, theology, philosophy and particularly spirituality. He bought and read and reviewed books almost to his last hour. But the bedrock of his faith remained the same. He was convinced that the only answers for a suffering and sinful world lie in the life and crucifixion-resurrection of Jesus Christ, the supreme gift to this world from a loving God who is also the creator and sustainer of all the worlds there are.

Beryl Wakefield, Lichfield 2002

VI

St John may speak of the Spirit coming as a dove, but the truth is that the peace and mercy and gentleness of the Holy Spirit may be more terrible than the forces of nature or the wrath of man. For the judgement of love is more fearsome than the perils of land or sea or air, or anything that human justice can do. In the end the Spirit consumes evil utterly and demands to set our whole being aflame with love.

Healed wounds are not necessarily disfigurement – 'With what rapture /Gaze we on those glorious scars'. The fact that his glorified body still has the wounds means that when Jesus rose from the dead the whole of his past rose with him. His sufferings were not forgotten though there was no spirit of vindictiveness - the wounds in some sense made him what he was. God made man, for man to die, wounded for our transgressions bruised for our iniquities, by whose stripes we are healed.

In society and in the Church, extraordinary and ordinary people support one another. It has been said that ordinary people are 'divinely ordinary'. Never think you are of little value or uncalled of God if you have no outstanding gifts. Moses brought water gushing from the rock he smote. You may gently offer the cup of water which the Lord has blessed.

The Eucharist is not only the ring on the Church's finger, it is the dagger at her heart. Here God in Christ says 'Your money and your life'. Here there may be given to you also old Simeon's warning to Mary 'A sword shall pierce your heart' Here love itself may pierce you with the sheer intensity of Christ, as many of the saints have found. Here you learn to take the wounds you receive not simply from enemies or from fate, but as part of the Divine healing from the wounded Christ.

Many of us know people who are always expressing the same doubts and difficulties. Year after year, interview after interview, house group after house group. They never get beyond them. And they should be treated with respect. They may be sincere pilgrims all the same, for faith would not be faith if there were no doubt and it were easy. There is a danger that we may cling to our doubts because they are our own. We have to learn that somehow we ourselves must be got out of the way, even by losing those experiences and convictions most precious to us, so that from the knowledge and love which is *grasping* we come to see that which is *giving*, a total oblation of ourselves through the sacrifice of Christ.

The Christian seeker may be a pilgrim rather than an explorer, travelling towards a goal, the goal of Christ's teaching on prayer. He or she may also be travelling along a Way which is Christ, in company with the saints. This does not mean a motorway along which one drives at speed ignoring the countryside and the conurbations. It is a journey on foot, painful and hazardous at times, but with eyes open, observant of nature and human nature and not indifferent to some terrible scenes, or reluctant to stop and help those in need, the victims by the wayside.

The Church is always in the wilderness in this world, and thereby never static, always moving on, painful and tragic as it often is to leave familiar and beloved scenes for new and harsher terrain. But there is a stubborn and recalcitrant belief that however great the hardships, disappointments and false hopes, we are marching towards the promised land and God has some better thing for us. The Church though so imperfect and pathetic is an absolute necessity, not as a sign set above the nations but as 'the poor Church of sinners, the tent of the pilgrim people pitched in the desert amid all the storms of history'.

Spirituality demands social embodiment The life of worship and prayer is not an escape from harsh realities; it does not dispense us from social and political action, from opposing racism and exploitation, from fighting for justice for 'all creatures great and small'. It may bring more disturbance than peace, more suffering than ease. There may be nought for our comfort. The 23rd Psalm is preceded by the 22nd - the good shepherd of green pastures and still waters, by the cry of forsakenness.

The Church is in fact distinguished from all other institutions because Christ loved it and gave himself as a bridegroom for his bride –for better for worse, for richer for poorer, in sickness and in health even to death. And it is that which brings us to the Lord's table, to think more of Christ's love than of our follies and failures.

Pope John 23rd was once at his wit's end about the Church when he heard Christ saying to him "Don't forget it's my church, Johnny" and as for the church so for its members. Do we come simply abandoning ourselves to God in Christ? Sometimes our guilt and terrible sense of failure and misspent years even in Christ's service may be a sign of egocentricity, self-absorption. We are concerned even in the holiest relationship chiefly with ourselves, whereas all that matters is Christ's love. This is my body given for you – for the church - and you.

I have a notion about Thomas. Was his doubt largely self-doubt? Was he not in deep distress, ashamed of himself, totally in despair about his own salvation? Is there not a parallel with Martin Luther, wondering if he could be saved, if he were not destined for damnation? And is not the advice he needs that which Luther's confessor gave him –"Leave such thoughts and begin with the wounds of Jesus". This is what Thomas would seek to do. He's heard testimony of Christ risen from the dead for judgement, on him not least. "If only I could see the wounds" Herein is our salvation.

In the Magnificat, Mary says that her spirit rejoices 'in God my Saviour.' But the whole song is about justice for God's people. Mary's salvation means theirs, freedom from oppression, food for the hungry, good news for the poor. And that is the truth about salvation, deliverance. It is personal, mine, in relation to the whole human race. I am not truly saved while people are exploited, abused, or hungry.

Our Lord bids us ask for the necessities of life. We do not take our substance as a right, we pray for it – do not snatch and grab. We recognise God's kingly rule and our dependence on him. And because all things come from God, all things are sacred. When the Jews blessed bread – and remember Jesus was a Jew- they were not making it holy. It was already that because it was God's before it was theirs. In blessing they were transferring it to their use, getting permission if you like, to take and eat.

Gather up the fragments that remain (John 6 verse 12). This injunction to collect the pieces left over applies also to our individual lives. The work of grace in our hearts may seem to have left us with nothing but fragments. And this not only in old age. Brokenness, waste, may be just as much the experience of youth. We must always be gathering up our resources which we have from God's bounty to offer back to him, even if they be but crumbs. And this must go on through our lives. Whatever our regrets, our failures or sense of futility and brokenness, we must never feel we have nothing to gather up for God.

Jesus came to Nazareth where he had been brought up (Luke 4 verse 16) They rejected him at Nazareth; he came to his own and they received him not. They rejected him everywhere in the end. To follow this programme of glorious hope for all mankind means for all Christ's followers the possibility of misunderstanding, obloquy, pain perhaps even martyrdom. It is hard to achieve worldly salvation with the methods of heaven. Hard for people hungry and oppressed in this world not to think that the end is for everyone to grow rich and have the benefits of material prosperity. The promise of their real treasure in heaven where Christ is, demands great faith.

We need to be for one another not spiritual directors, but soul-friends; not lords of faith but helpers in joy. To lay aside our garments- to strip ourselves of outward dignity, not so much the paraphernalia of office as of our supposed saintliness, and take a towel and pour water into a basin, to perform for one another that courtesy –for such it is- which carries assurance that our journey through the world does not make us unfit to eat and drink in the Father's house.

There is a truth unique to the Christian faith, that while God has put into our hearts a hunger for him, his kingdom and his righteousness, and we must be ever seeking those, ever pilgrims of perfection, God himself in Christ is seeking us, and to find is not so much our discovery as 'to be found of him'. And if our quest is often hard, it is as nothing to his: for he finds us and our humanity only in his death.

The Christian will indeed pray for right political judgement and exercise the duties of citizenship. But no political programme is a blueprint for the kingdom of God, and though Christians must not be above political engagement according to their opinions and conscience, they will know that they are never more under judgement than when so involved, never more in danger of conforming to the spirit of the age than being transformed by the Spirit of God.

In the reading of Holy Scripture we need many aids – men and women of letters, those with poetic imagination, those with a sense of history and tradition, who will feed us with the interpretation of the past, and those who will not let us escape from the text and the questions it poses and the demands it makes on our faith, its stresses and strains as well as its comforts and consolations.

These days there is much deprecation of the *word* –our worship contains too much talk, we need more visual aids, bodily movement. Yet the power of speech and hearing is unique and I do not think our hearts can be moved without some word -not turgid loquacity nor a bullying barrage, but some assurance conveyed by the Holy Spirit, put into words. "And his that gentle voice we hear".

Intellectual doubts are not the real trouble – they are defences which we erect, because we're half afraid of what religion may do to us and to our hearts. If we once get into that stable, if we once gaze on that Cross, who knows what may happen? *Hearts have fared strangely here/Don't be surprised should the love flame seize it/ Burn it and break it and wrest it from your keeping/Never to be yours any more.* That's what Christ does to you: no wonder you hesitate.

God does not give us visible certainty, 'we can see through a glass darkly', we live in the shadows of the world. He does not give us thunder and earthquake and lightning – but he gives us a voice, the voice of Jesus. The Gospels give us little idea what Jesus looked like –that was not the Jewish way. But they tell us about his heart, his compassion, his sternness and his voice 'Never man spake like this man'.

The crowds marvelled at the gracious words that proceeded out of his mouth. The centurion said 'Lord I am not worthy –speak but the word' Mary in the garden recognised him by the voice as he spoke her name. And we still have the voice of Jesus. God speaks to us as we read the Bible in the fellowship of the Church, in the Church throughout the ages. For a voice is a sign of life, it brings with it the possibilities of personal encounter.

A *Syrian ready to perish was my father* (Deut 26 verse 5).   When the Israelite of old appeared before God with the offering of the first fruits he was charged not to recall 'the glories of his blood and state,' but the fugitive Jacob sending his sons for alien corn, and their deliverance not by their own hand but by the hand of God. So it is with Christians. We have nothing to plead of ourselves. If we have any good deed or thought it is the Lord's doing. Our prayer is ever that of the publican 'God be merciful to me a sinner' – no one can outgrow penitence.

The Church, the covenant people of God, is in the world as a sign of his mercy. And that is our calling when the forces of nature and the wrath of man seem to deny God, the little struggling fellowship of pardoned sinners, impoverished and imperfect as it is, holds fast the banner of the Crucified and proclaims God's mercy for our troubled race.

M oses received a greater revelation of divine glory than most. And to some of us, irrespective of our place in the world, or education, or secular achievement, this may not be denied. There may be - there should be- more for us in Christianity than conventional religion, duty, respectability, an unimaginative down to earth worship confined to that narrow passage between the cradle and the crematorium, unaware of the sheer wonder of life with God, which transcends even death.

If the life of the world to come means the vindication of God, it also means the vision of God. We see him as he is, in the glory which we can hardly bear, but which draws us to him so that we cannot look anywhere else, and are lost in his immensity; so that we no longer have any interest in ourselves and desire nothing but to give ourselves to him, as he gave himself for us.

There is a saying of the French novelist Flaubert 'Real life is always misrepresented by those who want to make it lead up to a conclusion. God alone may do that: the greatest geniuses have never concluded'. The Resurrection is the act of God which does transcend human reason and scientific knowledge. It alone brings tragedies and disasters and fears of our fragmentary and mortal life to a grand AMEN.

The poet and the musician especially depend on an unaccountable power, part exquisite anguish, part rapturous joy which takes possession of them, and disciplined by craftsmanship brings forth art. Without this inspiration craftsmanship alone results in competence and nothing more. "Take not thy Holy Spirit from me". The preacher, crude and humble though his efforts are in comparison, is an artist in that he cannot preach without inspiration. A sermon must be more than an exercise in communication.

Jesus is no longer with us as a human friend because he has gone to God from whom he uniquely came. He is not just "Rabboni, my Master" as for Mary Magdalene, or even "My Lord and my God" as for Thomas. He belongs to God and to the innumerable millions of the human race in every age –in Africa, China and Soviet Russia as much in first century Palestine as in his Church today. And he is my Master and my Lord because he is the everlasting Son of the Father.

Our ministry is the gift of the Ascended Christ to the church and to the world. "Now the word ascended implies that he also descended to the lowest level". (Ephesians 4 verse 8) The Christian dimensions are vertical as well as horizontal and the symbol of our ministry is not the lotus flower nor the Buddha reclining, but the Incarnate, the Crucified stretched between earth and heaven. And if we derive a raison d'etre from the ascended Christ we are also followers of the one who first of all descended, emptied himself and took the form of a servant.

Eating and drinking is the way to our becoming like Christ. 'Man is what he eats' said the philosopher Feuerbach disparagingly, reducing humanity to mere matter. But that is the truth spiritually. As we feed on Christ in our hearts by faith with thanksgiving, we grow into the love his passion revealed, his death realised. When Jesus said to his friends over the bread 'This is my body' he meant this is my whole self, not simply the carnal part of me; and over the cup 'this is my blood', he was giving his life for them. And that is what he says to you and offers you.

When we remember those who have died, the veil of separation is very thin in Christ and it is not wrong to think that there may be still a mutual influence, and that we should seek to live the lives of sacrificial love which constitute their blessedness and their salvation too. Love is strong as death and reaches beyond it. We must indeed give them to God, for they are his before they are ours.

In the place where he was crucified there was a garden (John 19 verse 41)

There is a theory that St John mentions the garden because, as in the prologue to his Gospel, he has Genesis and the first creation and fall in mind. Here through what the Divine gardener has achieved on the Cross is paradise restored. There is an apparent gardener in John's account, but this is Mary Magdalene's mistake. It is Jesus. The garden is far more glorious than Eden, for here Adam/humanity will attain to divinity.

Wesley's hymn 'O Thou who camest from above' includes ' To work and speak and think for thee'. Notice 'and think'. Anti–intellectualism which one detects with alarm is no friend to Christian faith. Thinking should be joy, like physical athletics. It can be dangerous. It is hard work and it makes us confront doubts and not whistle them away. It may challenge our established convictions. It may mean we go through spiritual darkness. And yet faith should emerge stronger by thinking...always addressed to God, always part of our prayer.

An Orthodox theologian declared it is the energies of God, of his goodness and love which we partake; not his essence, the mystery of his inmost being, which is ineffable, beyond all knowledge, the understanding of our limited minds, the attainment of our human wills. But we are called to *Christlikeness*, itself the gift of God's grace, not our effort.

Where we as natural human beings encounter failure, frustration, disappointment, death, God the triumphant lover offers us himself and with himself all things. Then and then only do we apprehend possibilities entirely new, a knowledge of God that consists in being known; a love of neighbour created by God's death for him, the Abba Father voiced by the Spirit of Christ. Our only hope is not in natural cheerfulness, or glib optimism, or even in the beauty of the earth and 'laughter and the love of friends.' It is in the crucifixion-resurrection of Christ.

We have to go on living, not in a world of quasi-miraculous interventions, much less fairy tales, but amid harsh realities, in which the only unambiguous power we are given is that of self-sacrificing love. And yet it is this which enables us to ascend as on Christ's cross to the eternal life which is his with the father.

The Cross was not just the act of an obedient man who would not turn from what he believed to be his hour. It was the act of God, the supreme revelation of what God is eternally. He is no angry potentate demanding the sacrifice of his son to turn away his wrath. He is always love, pouring himself out in life and sacrifice. And the Holy Spirit is the love which dwells in the heart of God.

Lazarus stumbles out of the tomb bound hand and foot, blindfolded by the head cloth until Christ sets him free. (John 11 verse 44) It is all different from the resurrection of Jesus. He cannot be bound but goes his way leaving the grave clothes folded. It is almost as though John is saying that the raising of Lazarus is not 'the real thing'. Lazarus is restored to human life and love, but one day he will die again and no voice will call him from the tomb. This is an episode which must take place in order that the substance as well as the shadow of Divine omnipotence may be shown.

Discipleship is more than simply being a follower of Jesus, being his servant, obeying his commands. It is union with him and the Father, what Protestant writers have called mystical union. It is the result of the divine indwelling, of each Christian being one of the mansions in the Father's house. "Anyone who loves me will heed what I say: then my Father will love him and we will come to him and make our dwelling with him"

If a rational argument is required, I would claim that Christianity unites contemplation and action. It takes seriously both rough crude history and eternal verities and it is convinced that human life is of incalculable value to God. And, as Simone Weil said, its extreme greatness "lies in the fact that it does not seek a supernatural remedy for suffering but a supernatural use of it". For all these reasons I am still able to say " I believe."

The grim reality of evil everywhere, of demonic forces ever at work, is nothing to the saving mercy of our God whose Son loved me and gave himself for me. It cannot withstand the potency of what is given in the Holy sacrament. Not all the furies and torments of nature or of the human heart, or our worse than bestial crimes, not Winter's cold or Summer's heat, or Spring's tempests or Autumn's devastation, not plague, earthquake, famine, or tumult of war can prevail against a few drops of wine and some scraps of bread.

J esus bade us see the Father's providential care in the little things around us, birds and flowers, and taught the impartiality of nature, the ways of him who makes his sun to rise and his rain to fall on the just and unjust alike. But the rainbow symbolises the Divine mercy because it comes out of storm. It is no calm beauty mocking the violence and disaster of the world. And maybe it is only as we face the realities of sorrow and destruction and disaster that we understand what mercy means and how God's salvation is always from the edge of the abyss, from near tragedy.

"There is a cup in the hands of the Lord and the wine is red".

The wine God gives in Scripture is sometimes a deadly drink, the cup of his anger. But the Christian Gospel transforms all human experience because it transforms our knowledge of God through the Passion of Christ. The cup of suffering, the cup of blessing and the cup of Communion are all mysteriously the same cup. And if we enter the depths not simply of Israelite history, but of Christ's, find our place in his story, we shall, even in the worst sorrows, drink with him the royal wine of heaven.

When a Christian reads Isaiah's description of the Lord high and lifted up, there is a double meaning. He thinks not only of the awesome exaltation of the divine majesty in his unchanging perfection, but of the one who was lifted up on the cross, in which the writer of the Fourth Gospel bids us see also the ascent into heaven and the return to the glory which Christ has with the Father before all worlds. "As Moses lifted up the serpent in the wilderness so shall the Son of Man be lifted up". That refers to the crucifixion, the cross, a few feet above the heads of the gawping jeering crowds, but also the Son raised to the very height of heaven to change the whole perspective of the lives of his followers, so that now Christian lives take their character not from their circumstances ,but from his, and we live the heavenly ,the eternal life here and now.

Philip Martin, priest and poet who died in 1981,once wrote a poem in which he related the live coal of Isaiah's vision to Holy Communion. "Lo this hath touched thy lips". And it is the Holy Spirit who conveys the burning love and power of Christ's passion and risen life into the bread and wine. When Communion next touches your lips will you receive the searing pardon of God, your heart "wounded with love and joy", your vocation rediscovered, so that you too, abandoned to divine providence say "Here am I, send me".

You and I are humble instrumentalists in the orchestra of Christ playing the work of God. This is a way to understand prayer. It may sometimes be solo and lonely as Gethsemane. Some may feel in the homely phrase that they have a private line to the Almighty and indeed every believer has immediate access to the presence of God. But prayer is also our part in the divine symphony of the universe. And we – even we, such blundering participants - shall deprive the whole if we are missing or fail to tune our instruments at Christ's door.

Behind the appurtenances of religion we may be conscious of the ineffable reality. But how vague it all is! We have feelings, shivers down the spine maybe, we are even transported out of this world, but is it really God who is with us and are we taken to his abode? And there is nothing more profane and hypocritical than the way in which we testify to God's presence when the explanation may be simply psychological and we confuse the heartiness of good fellowship or the soothings of sentimental music with the direct apprehension of awesome majesty.

Many of us in childhood have a strong moral sense. This becomes weakened through the indulgences and compromises of later life. Our judgements are confused, our behaviour befuddled. We have lost our singleness of heart. If so we need to sit at the feet of the boy in the temple, even more to kneel before the man, founding the new temple on the cross: to refresh our jaded souls at the springs of his everlasting innocence and truth.

The cry of Dereliction "My God, my God, why have you forsaken me" may be according to St Mark, the last word of Jesus in his earthly life. But it is not the last word of God the father. As Jesus dies the veil of the temple is torn in two from top to bottom. There is now entry for all into the holy place. God is accessible in his free love to all people, and the Roman centurion, Gentile and pagan, comes first to faith. Already the King of Glory has overcome the sharpness of death and opened the Kingdom of heaven to all believers.

Christ's robe is still in tatters. The movement for Christian unity in our time has secured some notable triumphs and some signal reconciliations among the Churches who affirm the historic creeds. But all is not yet well even there. Here indeed is cause for tears and that deep sorrow and penitence which never seem to afflict some Christians in their glib, complacent certainties. Perhaps the remedy is in the simple fact that the taking of the robe by the soldiers means that he was stripped. He hung on the Cross between heaven and earth, naked. Our Christianity begins, not in our wealth of resources or ideas, not in our supposed knowledge of God, or our experience, not in what we may think we have done or can do for the kingdom, but in ourselves being stripped as he was. "Nothing in my hand I bring/Simply to thy Cross I cling".

C hristianity needs clothing and institutions in the world, and they may well add to the beauty of life. I cannot wish for all historic buildings to be pulled down or left to decay, or for the Gospel not to be preached in music and art. Iconoclasm no more serves God than Mark Antony's mob. But the work of God begins in the nakedness of Christ and in the admission of our own poverty. Only then are we given the new robe of righteousness, our nakedness covered by his grace.

Do you love me more than all else? When Peter says yes, Jesus goes on "Feed my lambs". Love of Christ and love of those who are his cannot be separated. If you love the shepherd you must love the flock; a lesson as hard as it is familiar. It may not be too difficult to love Christ, our ideal, our hero, our image of perfection, but those he brings with him? *Do you love me? And if you do, you have a responsibility for those who are mine, however contemptible, or uncongenial, culturally, racially, temperamentally different.* That is the message of the Easter Gospel, not only for Peter who had failed dramatically and been restored, but for you, who are no Peter, yet one with whom Christ has broken bread.

C an we understand who we are unless we know where we have come from? Can we ignore the past? Are we not in partnership with those who have lived and struggled then as well as with the future. What of Christian belief in the communion of saints? We diminish our lives and those of our contemporaries if we do not remember those who fought for our freedom and to preserve the eternal verities in our society.

Foot washing is not best done by a Pope or a monarch symbolically washing the feet of beggars. It is something we do for one another. Rank, even priestly orders are laid aside. A Methodist scholar once saw the equivalent in the Methodist class meeting, which was a group confessional; though he realised that for some a group would be no help, and confession should be made, and absolution received, the dirt wiped off, one to one.

What you and I must remember is that the Empty Tomb is witness to the cosmic implications of Christ's resurrection. It was not simply a spiritual experience. It was an objective act of God outside the hearts and minds of Christ's followers which involved the whole realm of nature, the physical universe, rocks and hills and farthest stars, what science reveals as well as the thought of the theologians or the experience of the humble poor.

We here and now in this world are citizens of heaven, or as Moffatt's translation has it 'We are a colony of heaven' Its not simply that we are on our way to God and the life of the world to come with passports in our pockets. No, in some ways we entered that life at our baptism. And now in this world we are representatives of the eternal kingdom, citizens of heaven already and colonists on earth. Never forget that. Our membership in the world to come is already secure in Christ.

The great promises of God are recorded in 2 Peter 1, verse 3 and 4). Hold fast to the promises. Sometimes rest in them, but remember we are pilgrims. Take courage even if your heart condemns you and you feel your only prayer is that of the publican 'God be merciful to me a sinner'. You were made in the image of God, and it is your destiny not simply to kneel afar off in helplessness and shame, but to share in his very being 'fullness of love, of heaven of God'.

Death is a cruel enemy, the ultimate change and separation. But for the Christian out of death comes life, new life, not the mere continuation of the old, nor its extinction either for the world is not all evil, nor our humanity an empty void. Robert Browning wrote 'God unmakes but to remake, he else just made in vain'. Evil is defeated, destroyed forever, but love lives eternally and takes into itself our pain and transforms it into a joy all the more glorious because there is the memory of suffering borne and overcome. This is the resurrection that is Christ.

For the beloved disciple at the empty tomb, there is no angelic presence, no appearance of a risen Jesus, no recall of Old Testament scripture from which some deduction might have been made of a Divine victory. He has but the empty tomb and the grave clothes. And these alone convince him. Only a mystic would have been brought to faith by emptiness. Yet it is when God seems to have withdrawn any signs of His presence that the mystic believes more than ever in His reality.

You cannot remove the paradox of Palm Sunday from your life. Have you come to terms with the King on a donkey who is also the white horseman of the Apocalypse, the Prince of peace who bears a sword? Have you attained that knowledge of God which destroys the idols and demons of your fear and brings you to the glorious liberty of the children of God? Do you fling wide the gate of your heart to the lowly Jesus and sing Hosanna though he may make war on your most cherished securities? Are you ready to cry Blessed is he who comes in the name of the Lord?

We cannot be other than men and women of our generation, whom the future will doubtless criticise for our blindness and lack of vision. All we can do is to follow Christ the servant as his servant, and the servant of others. But even though the one who follows sees only the back, and we may wonder where on earth Christ is going as the cross still bars his path, he may in the end turn and look on you and me and show his face of Divine compassion and say 'Well done good and faithful servant, enter into the joy of your Lord.'

There is one truth of the incarnation which is both our comfort and our challenge. Angels may leave us, esoteric experiences be illusory or not sustained. We may find it hard to make contact with Christ in prayer, but he does come to us in our fellow men and women. True, human relationships can be the most idolatrous of all. But without confusing human and divine, we ought in every encounter even the least attractive ask, "What may I see of Christ in him or her? Is there some revelation of the Son of Mary, the one who was crucified dead and buried and who rose on the third day?"

Should we not love God more after each Communion? It may not always feel like it, but be an empty ritual done out of not over-willing duty. Or worse we may leave the intense devotion and be very irritable, churlish even to our fellow worshippers and above all to our families. We may have been in heaven, but earth afterwards is an anticlimax and we cannot come to terms with its frustrations. It is easier to love God whom we have not seen with all the riches of his grace, than our neighbour whom we have. May God through the love shown on Calvary give us the desire to love him in return and our fellow human beings in him.

Our unity begins in God who is one, not simply that he is over against the multiplicity of idols "gods many and lords many", though there is courage and comfort to be gained from that. He is one in himself in the union of perfect love, expressed as that of Father and the Son. All our Christian life begins and ends there, not in Church order nor in the peace of the Eucharist, nor in the comradeship of mission, but in the unity of God. It is love as he is love. The love of the Father for the Son before the foundation of the world, embraces the disciples.

The theology behind the hymn *Love Divine, all loves excelling* is magnificent. Let me describe it in modern terms. God is love in his inmost being, and this love by its very nature he cannot keep to himself. It is poured out prodigally, unreservedly in creation, and he would share it with all his creatures, even you and me. He wishes them to be like him in his loving, he wants them to enter into his glory. And for this he has sent his very self in Christ "Joy of heaven to earth come down". Human beings may not be able wholly to receive this love because of sin; that barrier needs to be broken down, God's pardon secured by Christ's death and rising again.

Bethlehem cannot be sundered from Calvary. The conception and birth of Jesus are the start of a journey from manger to cross, and yet ends on the throne of the worlds. And this is the revelation in human life history of the eternal life of God. The *kenosis*, the self emptying we see in Jesus is not only a dateable event in time, it is of the Divine nature. For God in his perfection and eternal joy is forever pouring himself out in that sacrificial love, which subjects itself to evil, abandonment and death. And thence, only thence, the victory.

Each age is now equally near to Jesus and to the mystery of his passion. And indeed for us the historical and the eternal are inextricably fused together. We have both the Jesus of history and the Christ of faith, the faith of so many down the centuries. We are more privileged than those on Easter evening or Thomas the week after. "Blessed are those who have not seen and yet have believed." This is no discipleship at second hand.

If as Christians we are supposed to live 'for' others, the fact is that we live 'from' others as they do from us. It is a matter of exchange. We cannot be made perfect apart from them and they from us. All Saints Day teaches us that in Christ above all we are members one of another. We in our generation and particular circumstances are part of the whole body of Christ, world without end.

An ancient thanksgiving prayer of the Church says 'He opened wide his arms for us on the cross'. In the fourth century Athanasius asked 'Why did Jesus die on the cross and not some other way?' and answered 'because only on a cross does one die with outstretched hands; and with one Jesus embraced the ancient people the Jews, and with the other all the peoples of the world'.

Perhaps those of us who seek to serve Christ need to go in the spirit, and led by the spirit into the desert, to recover our hunger and thirst for God, to escape the dizzy distractions of a confused world with too many options, and to discover singleness of heart. To find again in the austerity of the open wind swept places the vision which is our beatitude. And if you say the vision given in the desert may be a mirage, I can only reply 'Not if it has about it the outlines of a place called Calvary, not if it reveals a divinity which in all its suffering is for us men and for our salvation'.

'Behold I make all things new' says the one who sits on the throne. And this transfigures both the whole tragedy of human life and, as in Keble's hymn 'the trivial round, the common task'. Mercy is all around us, ever new and ever young; we may be 'surprised by joy' as though we were present at first creation, or denizens already of the eternal kingdom. Christ's sacrifice releases God's love into all the world. It gives his body and his blood to be our daily sustenance and inspiration. His mercies are new every morning of the world and of your life, but never more than on the dread morning when Christ bore his cross to Calvary.

There is a hint in the Gospels that Mary may have been reluctant to let go of her son, probably always aware of him as the little boy of Nazareth or even the baby in her arms. This may be the meaning of the incident in which she and his brothers try to reach him through the crowd. (Luke 8 verse 14) Here is a lesson for the Church. We cannot possess and domesticate and tame Jesus, or confine him to what we consider his natural kinship in blood or even spiritual succession. He is greater than we and goes his way free of ecclesiastical control or theological definition. He has a wider family than that which has an apparent right to claim him. 'Not everyone who says to me "Lord, Lord" shall enter into the kingdom of heaven, but he who does the will of my father who is in heaven'.

Do not let us minimise the cost, not simply of Christ's sufferings physical and mental, but of making himself part of continuing history. He did not throw himself down from the temple parapet, nor descend from the cross, but he cast himself into the muddied stream of history, which would at times be further polluted in consequence of the deeds and attitudes of those who professed devotion to him and claimed to be guardians of his truth.

Faith must safeguard the mystery of God and not claim that it can explore the utmost depths of his being or manipulate him to its own conceived advantage. This is why there must be paradox in faith. God is both revealed to faith and hidden, known and yet unknown. He is light and yet clouds and darkness surround him. He is omnipotent, almighty yet we see him only in the powerlessness and weakness of Christ's cross. He is all holy, 'of purer eyes than to behold iniquity' and yet receives sinners and is one with the men and women he created.

It is a poignant fact that in history many who sow precious seed do not see the harvest. All has to be in faith. We reap the harvest sown by others, for which we have not laboured. But in Christian reality, in the sight of God, the sowing and the reaping are one, so that there is no discouragement or jealousy but one shared and equal joy. And all because the sowing of Christ himself in death annihilates time and brings us even now in this very moment amid all our toil and uncertainty, the barrenness and stony ground and our own transience, to the harvest home of eternal life and love.

A purpose of silence is to enable us to listen, though too often we retreat into our introverted musings; it is also to enable us to speak, to utter the word that comes from our attention to God and to other people. This, and not mystic absorption, was the original intent of Quaker silence. And for us silence should open our minds, deliver us – though often by much wrestling – from our prejudices, censor our words, edit and abridge them, but help us to communicate God's truth and love. In the end we shall discover not simply that words are inadequate, we shall be caught up in a rapture of praise, and in anticipation of the worship of heaven : *"Sing and stop and gaze and fall/ O'erwhelmed before thy throne"*.

We must not deceive ourselves into thinking that because prayer and life for the Christian should be one, that there is no need to set aside time apart for prayer. Though God holds us in existence whether or not we hold him in consciousness, we shall never know him, nor become the means by which his grace reaches others, unless we open ourselves to him – with words or without –and think about him with the help of Holy Scripture and the great tradition of the saints. We are no use as empty vessels even if they do make the most noise; we need to be reservoirs, filled to the brim and overflowing if we are to refresh the life of parched and thirsty humanity.

It is a truism of modern psychology that it is often the guilty person who commits the crime. A sense of sin may precede the evil deed. Because you feel you are a miserable offender, you will offend. In our worship and our living we need to be lifted above our sins into the world of Christ's triumph and to be encouraged to the boldness of the apostle: 'I can do all things through Christ who strengthens me'

There is need for the penitent within the saint. And is this not what we find in Christ, very God of very God without sin and yet the perfect penitent? United with Christ in his sacrifice for the sins of the world, we go on to live our Christian lives, 'ransomed, healed, restored, forgiven'. But we could not be ransomed if we had never been enslaved, could not be healed unless we had been sick, could not be forgiven if we were not sinners. And tears can only be wiped away from eyes which have been filled with them.

The life death and resurrection of Jesus are the demonstration in time and history of the eternal character of God. The Lord of creation is also the servant of his creatures. He forever stoops from his heavenly throne to perform the most menial tasks for our good, to do the chores of his own universe. The hands that fashioned heaven and earth bring us cleansing from the pollution of our natures 'all the filth of sin and pride'. They offer us part with him in the glory of his own being and the work of redeeming love which is greater than the making of the worlds.

This is God's world. The earth is the Lord's, not the landlord's, nor the war lord's. And not this world only but all the worlds there are. All were made to fulfil his purpose, 'his mercy's whole design'. Unless we believe that, we are in danger of falling into the superstitions which bedevil our society. We shall look for causes and explanations by consulting fortune tellers, or mediums or ouija boards or even taking half seriously the astrological columns of the popular press. We cannot ourselves bring in the kingdom, but we can prepare its way every moment of our lives, look for its signs even amid disaster and death and oppose evil and injustice with unconquerable hope.

We must never forget that the first New Testament before ever there were authorised Christian writings, was the cup of the new covenant in Christ's blood. But the Scriptures, which are essential to Christian worship, have the same effect. They make us one with the whole history of Christ from first creation to the end of time. As we hear the word we are there, contemporaries with the Church throughout all the world and throughout all ages, of that divine deed in which all humanity and all nature are redeemed.

The God of the Scriptures is, as Pascal discovered 'not the God of the philosophers and the scientists'. He is the God whose existence cannot be proved by rational argument, but who can be known; who may be addressed rather than expressed, the God who enters into living personal relationships with his children, who is at once our judge and our friend. He is the God who pours out his life and his love that his creatures may be partakers of his likeness. This enables us to persevere amid all vicissitudes, griefs and failures. This is what Paul means when he says that the God of the Scriptures is the God and Father of our Lord Jesus Christ.

It is true that the great classics of devotion, however different their origins in time, civilisation or theology, transcend denominational barriers. This is why some Catholics have felt 'at home' in *Pilgrim's Progress* and some Methodists these days find that the *Spiritual Exercises* of Ignatius Loyola provide a form of prayer which transforms their lives, as well as containing passages which remind them of the Covenant service. John of the Cross has affinities with Martin Luther and with Buddhism.

The Christian life is not a descent into irrationality. It is a quest for truth, yet truth is not simply mental; it involves the whole being; it is moral as well as intellectual. There is a difference between science and wisdom. And the true wisdom is gained by contemplation, a looking toward God with longing love and that concentration of the will which is purity of heart, and which for our distracted selves is hard to obtain.

We all mourn the ravages of time and change. So much goes, some things improve, others deteriorate, all change. We long for our youth, old companions, even for some past age of the world. But we have our Jesus. Here is no melancholy sigh, "if youth but knew, if age only could". This is the one relationship in life which can never be sundered. If Christ is gone from us and is hidden in the mists of distance or of doubt we may find him again as we try to become the vessels and instruments of his mercy even in the darkness of the world; for we have the promise of the one who comes with the clouds of heaven.

We cannot plumb the full depths of Christ's agony in the garden or on the cross. He flung himself into the torrent of his Passion with nothing but faith and love. And even now his victory in human lives and the nations of the world is only partial. The future may hold more crosses and failures. Yet even in the darkness of his bitterest woe there were gleams of light and joy and far off echoes of the music of heaven. So it may be for you.

I believe there are more mystics among so called ordinary Christians than they are prepared to admit. They are not necessarily intellectuals, but they have an access to God which scholars and academics and normally intelligent people find by a longer route which sometimes never ends. The only qualification is love. As Michael Ramsay once put it, all that is needed " is to try to be obedient and humble and to love God very much"

God does not speak his Divine word from paradise but from the flesh of a man born in a lowly stable, working in a carpenter's shop, wandering prophetically between Galilee and Jerusalem, crucified on an eastern hillside. We hear him amid the sufferings and the joys of human life. He speaks to all equally and not just to mystics, and the promise is ever the same: "My grace is sufficient for you, for my strength is made perfect in weakness".

Every time we come to Church hope should be rekindled. This is what the world so sorely needs and which is part of the Church's title-deeds. The command of Christ "Do this in remembrance of me" could mean "Do this that God may remember me and bring in his kingdom". At any rate Paul says that in Holy Communion we proclaim the Lord's death "until he come." It is a sacrament not only of memory, but of hope.

A preacher or any Christian giving testimony must always speak 'from the heart'. There must be underlying fervour or feeling, though it will not always be rhetorical. It must however be set in a 'heavenly' context, other-worldly in the sense that it is conscious of the eternal, that it offers a vision behind the mundane and the utilitarian 'getting and spending', short term temporal advantages. The expedient is transcended by the Kingdom of God.

What would be the result if we genuinely looked in our hearts to gain inspiration for our preaching and witnessing, personal relations, Christian lives? There may be some things of beauty even in a rag and bone shop, even objects which would surprise us if priced in the spiritual "Antiques Roadshow", but how much else ? We need to pray with Charles Wesley "Take my heart, *but make it new*".

Jesus whose praise has reached to the ends of the earth. Jesus, acknowledged in the Te Deum, in the Creeds, in the Orthodox liturgy, in the Latin Mass, in the Book of Common Prayer and in the new forms of our own day. Jesus, adored in the offices of monks and nuns "when the yews were young that made the bows for Agincourt", as now in the concrete jungles and shopping precincts. Jesus beloved of raucous Methodist field preachers singing Wesley hymns. Jesus, served to the last in prison camps and by those who will not acquiesce in racial inequality. Jesus the meek unspotted lamb, gentle and good bearing our sins, but the Christ also of Llandaff and Coventry, strong, majestic, our Judge; "Christ of revolution and of poetry". Jesus the crucified, risen, ascended, glorified, the same yesterday today and forever, the eternal Son, the way to the Father.

Christian worship always takes place on the battlefield of life. Jesus instituted the Sacrament on his betrayal night when 'his last and fiercest strife was nigh'. We ourselves may meet in a peaceful church in the society of our friends, but outside there are Rwanda, Bosnia, Northern Ireland, gang warfare violence and terrorism. Yet even in the shadow of atrocities and death, if humanly possible, Christians will gather round a table and fulfil Christ's command.

God "sees life steadily and sees it whole". This does not mean that he makes for us the excuses which we are all to ready to make for ourselves. He cannot condone the evil which he alone sees. Yet his mercy is infinite. He knows our circumstances, our heredity, our genes; that which makes the struggle against temptation hard. And this all the more because he has taken our nature upon him in Christ. Jesus looked on the rich young ruler and loved him, though of his free will he had rejected Christ's demand. Jesus looked upon Peter and his love broke Peter's heart.

For the disciples, eating with Jesus is essential. It is not only that Christ becomes their spiritual food. They who share his table fellowship are to be with him in the action of his sacrifice. They do not go with him to Calvary. He is crucified not between James and John, but two terrorists. His, and his alone is the full perfect and sufficient sacrifice for the sins of the whole world. And yet by the outward actions, eating the bread and drinking the wine, they are in the future, when their failure is past, to become one with him in his finished and continuing work. And so it is for us.

When we gather for worship with the minority which is the Church, we are not simply members of a society which gives us interest and friendship and on occasion entertainment. We are Christ's, both his people and as he is in the world. And in our Upper Room in which we learn the secrets of eternal life and are the friends of Jesus, we never forget the teeming multitudes of the world hungering for love and peace and justice, as sheep without a shepherd, whom Christ bids us feed with the bread of life.

C hrist is the universal Saviour and his death and resurrection are for all, even if they do not know him, or follow other paths to fullness of life. Other faiths do not appreciate this and regard it as one more instance of Christian imperialism. Although I do not proclaim this aggressively, it is what I believe in the depths of my being. The whole Christ is greater than the Jesus of history, though identical with him, and the resurrection like the cross is true of the eternal being of God.

The teaching of the Fourth Gospel about the indwelling of the Father and the Son with the believer, presages a mystical union of awesome intimacy. It is the fount of all consequent contemplative experience. It is the promise of the whole Christ, inseparably one with the Father, not simply enthroned over the worlds but in the very being of the disciples. But St John's is not a charismatic or solely spiritual Gospel. The Jesus who with the Father makes his abode in the believer is the Jesus of history, the Word made flesh.

Our God is the God of the desert, not the construct of our highest ideals and noblest thoughts, proved by our arguments or made manifest by our good behaviour. In some aspects he is strange, terrible, remote, hidden: yet he speaks to us out of the burning bush, the thunders of Sinai and the darkness of the Cross. And we must learn the lesson which Moses tried to teach his recalcitrant and rebellious people, that in the end we have only God, who will be what he will be, who alone can feed us and give us drink and lead us to the promised land.

A personal relationship is dynamic. So it may be with the soul and God. There will not be untroubled serenity. There may be times of complaint and doubt. As knowledge grows, understanding may change. One's view of God may alter. There may be what has been called 'a crucifixion of images'. The way in which we have conceived God may need to change. But finally there is conviction that this is the life of heaven below.

It is not always easy to play with our grandchildren in this age of computer games and television. But Christmas for example, must not be all theology, even though it is there that our comfort and salvation lie. The stable at Bethlehem was not a seminar, and if for a while we can lose ourselves and our intellectual and spiritual preoccupations in simple enjoyment and sharing young lives, we may not be far from the one who is forever the Holy Child Jesus.

I am inclined to agree with a doctrine endorsed by John Wesley that we are to consider ourselves particular objects of God's providence; "under the same care and protection of God as if the world had been made for us alone. It is not by chance that a man is born at such a time, of such parents and in such a place and condition". Please God we may echo Bonhoeffer's testimony " My life is full of God's mercies. And over all sin stands the forgiving love of the crucified."

The Holy Communion is the sacrament of the interval, of waiting, but more, it takes us to the heavenly places. As we eat and drink in union with our fellow Christians, " in love and charity with our neighbours" we are there. Time is rolled up and we are one with the angels and archangels and all the company of heaven. For those moments we are no longer in waiting, in suspense. All that God has done from the foundation of the earth is present before us " and the promise of our inheritance is sealed upon our wondering hearts".

A sentimental Jesus devotion does not do justice to the one, severe as well as kind, who confronts us in the Gospels. Yet it is important to remember that Jesus was a man, that he belonged to a particular culture, that in his youth he plied a trade, actually worked with the materials of the physical world. And that he surrendered everything, gave up a secure living, to follow what he believed to be the will of God. He was taken out of himself as a man, and also we believe as second person of the Trinity in his incarnation and he bids us follow his example of great humility.

The problem is not only with each daily page of our lives, but with the whole book. There may be in our lives past sins, which are as blots which penetrate and stain the whole and which cannot it seems be erased. We have sinned against God, who we believe forgives us if we are truly penitent, but we may have done irreparable damage to other people, injured them and our relationship for life. The only hope for us is a deliverance through a work not our own, the belief that Christ has made full atonement and that he represents our will for healing and binds up the wounds we have caused.

L ead us not into temptation. It seems contrary to Scripture to pray to be delivered from temptation for the Bible is the book of temptations from the beginning to end, from Eve and Adam in paradise to the Revelation of St John. Abraham is tempted to offer his only son on whom the promises rest. Job is tempted to the last extremity of cursing God. Jesus, after his baptism, is driven by the Holy Spirit he has just received to be tempted of the devil. And in each case the temptation is a test. Resistance strengthens the soul, it brings it to the supreme loyalty of faith in God against all human desires and loves.

This is my body - there is a wealth of meaning in the words of distribution at the Sacrament of Holy Communion. The essential meaning is the divine love. But I myself still want to pray in the words of the mediaeval Anima Christi "Body of Christ save me". They take me back to the historic Jesus, to what was done once for all on the cross, and yet which is ever present now, to what is given to me and yet is to be shared in the body which is the Church, and beyond in the whole body of our torn humanity.

Church buildings of various forms may be sacraments of God's presence, and additions to life's beauty. They may be theatres of his glory and what goes on inside should be for all communions. But it is the Spirit which alone matters – the love in our hearts for God and neighbour, the purity and singleness of heart, the longing to offer ourselves to God joined with the sacrifice of Christ through whatever forms there are. And the Spirit breaks down all barriers, destroys divisions, makes it possible whatever our outward practice for us to share in our hearts in the worship of all those who have loved Christ, the whole communion of saints.

Sight, physical or spiritual is one of the blessings of this life. It enables us to see the wonders of the world as well as its tragedies. Christians whose eyes Christ has opened have often experienced the world transformed. The supreme joy is not in nature, but in the eternal kingdom, which, when he had overcome the sharpness of death, Christ opened to all believers, and which we glimpse, though from afar. But we should never forget that the giver of sight to the blind, and hearing to the deaf, the bringer of the life of God to a dying world, did so as he made bread his broken body and wine his shed blood.

Liturgy is not a word which Methodists have used much until our own time. Literally the word means "the people's work" and in ancient Greece liturgy was a kind of income tax paid by the well-to-do in the form of public works. It might be salutary if, instead of complaining, we thought of income tax as our liturgy done for the common good. In Christian usage liturgy means an act of worship. "There is no such thing as a non liturgical church since liturgy is by etymology simply 'public service' and therefore the 'corporate worship' of any Christian community". But liturgy should be our life.

It is better to speak of eternal life than of immortality. This does not wait for death it begins here and now. In Colossians 3, Paul tells his Christian readers that they have already been raised with Christ. Resurrection is the term the New Testament prefers to immortality, for this takes the reality of death seriously, but affirms that it has been conquered and redeemed, so that it is not the last enemy, the end to all our hopes, the ultimate symbol of life's futility, but the entrance to eternal life. In one way or another we must all pass through it, but we do so as we follow Christ who *"leads me through no darker rooms than he went through before"*.

We must not live in constant recollection "of old unhappy far off things and battles long ago", as though the Battle of the Boyne were yesterday or Wesley's ejection from the Church a contemporary event. Nelson Mandela forgiving almost unforgivable injustice is an example to us all. And yet evil is a reality and error always possible. Although we must not brood on them and always see them against the background of Christ's passion, we must not forget the Holocaust or apartheid , Rwanda or Serbia. The human nature which we all share is capable of these things. We must learn to discern the evils which cannot be excused. Holiness denounces and repents and separates itself forever from "oppression, lust and crime".

We must affirm the first chapter of Genesis "God saw everything that he had made and it was very good". We have vigorously to contend for a good divine intention. It is a challenge to faith that must be met, that the purpose of this mysterious universe and human life within it, is good and goodness must in the end prevail. But this is not something that can be read off human or natural history. It is enough that goodness exists, is a reality, is evidenced every day and must never pass notice even while it is sometimes ambiguous and is accompanied by the evil in which so many involved in world events find it easier to believe. "My past life is replete with God's goodness, and my sins are covered by the forgiving love of Christ crucified".

There is the problem of the differences among Christians as to what basic Christianity is. I would say that it is the belief that both individually and in society we are to reveal the life of God as seen in Jesus Christ. Jesus himself is God's act or word, partly indeed the result of human evolution and the history of Israel, but supremely the gift of God's love for humanity and the universe. To this we must hold fast and for this we must contend.

What trust Jesus had in his first disciples! They never completely understood him. Peter though he repented of his denial and was restored, hardly showed the spirit of his Lord when, as leader of the church, he condemned Ananias and Sapphira. Yet somehow these men's proclamation of the gospel has endured. And now Christ leaves the task to us. It is an awesome responsibility and we often fail both in understanding his demands and living his love. But he has left his ministry to us.

In St John's Gospel the friends of Jesus are those who know the Father's will revealed in him. And they obey it. In our human friendships there is understanding, but obedience is what we owe to God. The unity of Christian people is achieved in answer to the prayer "Thy will be done" In seeking that, we find love for one another.

In our human experience the one who has fallen in love knows what it is to be pierced, though if love is to bring its transforming rewards it is necessary to settle down and not live in perpetual excitement or ecstasy, though the latter is something which Christians should experience from time to time. It is part of the life of heaven when we are taken out of ourselves and with all the saints are lost in God, and the wonder of his being and his love. In the infinity of the Godhead, there is a pierced human heart. And we find our eternal safety hidden in Christ's wounded side.

There may be but a handful of us gathered under one roof for worship, but there are in fact "angels and archangels and the whole company of heaven" a multitude which no man can number. And we never worship alone even when by ourselves. We are always part of a vast company, not only those who may be counted here on earth, but also of all those who have worshipped Christ and are still one with us in his indivisible fellowship. Our praises are joined to theirs for all eternity. In this sense *"The voice of prayer is never silent/Nor dies the strain of praise away"*.

Jesus has gone away that he may come again. The whole purpose of his departure through death and victory is to make possible a real Presence, more close, more intimate than anything conceivable before. The disciples are henceforth to be *united* with their Lord, so closely that they will be like branches of a vine or the eaters of bread. For the Christian Christ is not simply a figure of past history, nor is he God enthroned 'above' whatever that means – he is the atmosphere we breathe, the blood of our bodies, the life of our souls.

The friends of Jesus are those who know the mystery of the kingdom of heaven, or as Paul would say are privy to the whole counsels of God. But this does not mean dogmatic certainty or assurance; it does not enable you to answer all questions in earth and out of it. You won't pass your exams without the requisite ability and hard work. You will often walk in the dark, but the deeper the darkness the more you believe that you are on the road to the splendour of God. The disciples are not natural friends, kindred spirits, boon companions. They would not be together at all by natural affinities. They are there because Christ has called them.

The Spirit, promised to us, and so disturbing an influence, is our friend and inseparable companion, bringer of comfort, courage and conviction . We need to be disturbed by the realities of life and death; if we are not troubled by external anxieties we shall find our fears and conflict within. Some of the struggles which people used to have against the forces of nature, oppression and the shadow of death, which they feared, saved them from the ever increasing neuroticism of our time. But the gift promised by Jesus means that amid all confusion and hopelessness there is one within us, who troubles the waters, but also breathes peace and brings order out of the chaos.

The word Christ, the name of Jesus, is Greek and means the same as the Hebrew Messiah, the anointed one. Yet we are not told of Jesus being anointed by a prophet or a priest, only by three women at different times, or maybe in fact one and the same. He says very solemnly that he is being anointed for his burial, not for kingship for he is going to die. Yet his death shows us that God loves us and is merciful, that he forgives our sins and like the good Samaritan with the injured man at the roadside, pours oil into our wounds, the oil of healing, and gives us the peace of his living presence.

Now Jesus knew the story of the sacrifice of Isaac and so did his disciples – it was read at the Passover. And it is not contrary to the spirit of the New Testament to see in Isaac as well as Abraham what our fathers would call a type of Christ in his cross. Jesus willing to go to death, Jesus the victim, Jesus knowing intense agony, and yet in the end surrendering himself completely. But just as the sacrifice on Moriah was Abraham's as well as Isaac's, so the sacrifice of Calvary was God's. Those older thinkers were not wrong who saw the conflict of it – God's mercy pleading with his justice. But the conflict was not between the Father and his Son, the wrath of God and the compassion of Jesus. *"They went, both of them together."*

"He was already in the world."

This implies some doctrine of the pre-existence of Jesus Christ as the first chapter of John proclaims. Because though he and the events concerning him were particular, unique and decisive, they were glimpsed before whenever love gives itself for others. In the prophet Hosea loving his faithless wife; the suffering servant bearing the sins of his people; the very act of the creation, God speaking out his mercy in the whole universe and in showing that his very being is love, and that his life of bliss and majesty is not enough, he must pour out his very self in nature and humanity. So the Incarnation was the perfect manifestation of what had always been in the world and was the purpose of all life and history.

One meaning of Christ's act over the bread and wine in the Upper room is his attempt, by making his disciples eat and drink, to bind them to him whatever might happen, so that he would not have to go on his way alone. In fact they slept in the garden and had no part in the prayer 'Thy kingdom come', prayed as with a sweat of blood, then 'Thy will be done.' The kingdom did not come as at the consummation of the age. The sufferings of Christ and humanity are not over. Yet here is the rule of God in his commitment to the human race through the unswerving obedience of his Son, who will fulfil his mission of goodness and love and confrontation with evil to the last.

Remember whose voice spoke the Universe into being, who may be heard if only we will listen to the music of the planets and the whispers of the least of things. Remember him who above all has spoken in his Son and never more than when the Eternal lay speechless in the manger, or cried out forsaken on the cross. Remember him who raised Jesus from the dead and exalted him, not to leave us desolate but that he may fill all things. Remember him who is there at the end – the omega as well as the alpha, who is indeed the end of endings who will remain our life and joy and salvation when men and universes cease to be.

Discipleship is not an eternal triangle – it is a straight line of individual responsibility to Christ. God has called each one of us with our differing gifts, we each have something to offer him, something of our own. We ought to be so anxious to fulfil our obligations that we have simply no time to judge others. And if they stand condemned by pride or compromise, we must look to ourselves all the more, for who knows what the searcher of all hearts finds in us.

We forget that next to being a book about God the Bible is a book about sinners, and it seems the only people God is interested in are sinners –again and again in the parables Jesus makes this plain. The Prodigal, the Pharisee, the Publican – not a jovial landlord but a rascally tax gatherer, and what comes right home, the labourers in the vineyard. We demand rights and equality and the rewards commensurate with service rendered, and God laughs at us.

The presence of the Spirit is not to be judged by counting heads, but by growth in love, the suffering and sacrificial love of the Cross, the love which unites men and women with the life of God. I don't say that numbers do not matter or that one does not want to see an increase. Christianity could die out, at least in the forms of the past centuries. Yet the Spirit- filled church is one with an increase in love, not simply in numbers.

Evil *has* been overcome and we do not wait for a new revelation, nor is life an endless succession of Calvaries. There is one victory and one completed work – *but we have to identify ourselves with it.* "To show forth the Lord's death until he come" – to seek every day the power of his Cross. Every sin you ever committed can be nailed to his Cross. As you hear across the centuries the hammer blows, think of your sins being laid low – exposed and lifted up, drawn out from the hiding places of your excuses and forgetfulness, but triumphed over openly because Christ died to conquer your sins once for all.

It may be that you would not describe your discipleship as a constant living with Christ. You may not feel you know him as your earthly friend. You may feel you are far from being a mystic, or that the chief longing of your heart is to be lost in God. Ecstasy for you may be a happy family, God's love mediated through people. Do not despair. You have a mission none the less among those who may be uninterested or indifferent to what you do in Church. You may still show them in deeds and words what you believe God has done for you and for them and for all the world in the love revealed in Christ.

A s our sorrow is but for a while, so our deep joy once attained is independent of the changes and chances of this life. The joy in the Gospel promises has its source in Christ alone. It is a consequence of our committal to him. It is no frothy delight in the wonders of a Spring morning or in some human pleasure, God-given as these are. It rests entirely on the application to our hearts and lives of the objective and unalterable fact that Christ has triumphed over every thing that can assault or hurt our souls, for God has raised him from the dead.

Our hope is not based on anything we can do. A contribution to Christian Aid, a testimony to Christ's love in the ear of an unbeliever, a right political attitude- these may have some immediate effect in saving life and in the long term saving civilisation. But they will not make the world heaven nor bring back those who have died through human cruelty or incompetence. "Thou must save and Thou alone". And because we dare to affirm that God has done what is beyond all human endeavour we do not hold a memorial service for Jesus Christ. We look beyond the devotion of people to that power of love which in the similitude of an angel rolled away the stone from the sepulchre and made him the first-born from the dead.

Jesus, who is the cornerstone of the true temple of God is also the stone of stumbling to those who reject him. True the common people heard him gladly but only for a time. He puzzled them as much as attracted them to the last, and their misunderstanding was so great that he had to escape them and no vast movement of popular sympathy was with him at the end.

His Mother kept all these sayings in her heart. At times Mary's might have almost been the same question as John the Baptist's "Art thou he that should come or do we look for another?" This is a great problem for you and me. If those who saw and heard Jesus, even his mother, had their doubts what hope is there for faith for us. And yet if we understand the New Testament aright the fact is that our position is much more enviable, more advantageous than theirs, because we have the wholeness of Christ's work before us. They lived before Calvary and Easter when his task was still unfolding. We have heard the cry "It is finished". They saw the question mark "Who is this?" We see a Cross.

Jesus, the teacher, was himself the one most open to learn, always dependent on the Father, always obedient, always aware of the least of things; the sorrowful woman, the joyful child, the penitent sinner, the sheep gone astray, the coin lost, the seed sown in the earth. He compared himself even to this- 'except a corn of wheat fall into the earth and die, it abideth alone'. He was indeed the heavenly sower, casting the seed over hill and dale and on the last bare hill he sowed himself. The teaching of Jesus is found supremely not in the Sermon on the Mount but in the Cross on the Hill.

G lory is a word often used without understanding. Often we think of it as the tribute
and adulation which the dictator demands. Does
God want us to be forever paying him compli-
ments? But the word 'glory' contains almost the
whole Biblical revelation – God's power, his
character, the dazzling radiance of his majesty,
his accessibility, his nearness to us in Christ –all
these are summed up in 'glory'. And this glory
the whole of creation is to share. God's glory is
the vindication of his purpose in the Universe,
and the beatific vision which is the goal of every
individual's Christian life, to see God face to face.

In this world of war we need those who wait in peace; in a world of noise we need the silent; in a world where the resources of the earth are being squandered until they are all consumed, we need men and women who ask for no more than a place in which to pray, and make few demands for food and clothing; in a world of change when time, too, is interfered with and life is in danger of becoming a fantasia beyond human control, we need those who make again the old affirmation – our times are in God's hands.

Are we capable of loving God perfectly? Are we capable of loving him at all? The philosopher Ludwig Wittgenstein once said to a friend "You cannot love God, for you do not know him". Christians who are less agnostic, less philosophic have felt that our love is not worth considering, so tainted is it with selfishness and lustful desire. Yet the New Testament dares to say that 'We love because he first loved us' and sees our love as a response created by God's Holy Spirit, who sheds the love of God abroad in our hearts. God wants us to love him, to share his very self with us, to make us capable of his Divine perfection for he does not keep himself to himself, but rather would take us up into the torrent of love which is his Divine being.

Perfection is not a moral state which cannot be improved, but a constant growth in love to God and neighbour. Gregory of Nyssa, the Cappadocian Father says " This truly is the vision of God: never to be satisfied in the desire to see him". It is like the mountaineer who having reached one peak sees a whole range stretching before him, beckoning him on to fresh endeavour to fresh exhilaration and joy of reaching even greater heights. The perfection is in pressing on.

Confidence for the timid and inhibited comes from the same source as humility for the arrogant and over bold – dependence upon God.

If I am a strong and gifted man like Paul- and none of us can be on equal terms with him, by any standards he was one of the great personalities of world history, a man of towering might and energy - but if I have gifts and achievements to my credit then I need to know that none of these is in any way commensurate with what God has done for me in Christ, and that is the only ground of my strength. And if I am weak and frightened and conscious of my own failure – then also my confidence is in the grace of God which does its perfect work in such as me.

Within the Church there are often the most terrible divisions. Matthew (18 verses 10 - 20) has four lessons for congregations today. (a) A love for the 'little ones'. These are not necessarily children, though what our age has done to them must be a cause of deep penitence. It has often made them adults before they have learned the difference between right and wrong. (b) A concern for the 'lost' within the church as well as outside, and this with the compassion and patience of a good shepherd, not by censorious nagging, nor self-righteous rebuke. (c) Greater honesty and an ability to tell faults 'plain and home', with the recognition that we are not ultimate judges. Congregations must be prepared with infinite care and grief, to tell some people that 'they may walk no more with us'. (d) The value of the small group, not to bring pressure, or to be a cabal of the 'holier-than- thou' but to meet in the name of Christ wanting only encounter with him in the love he brings. This is the true church.

I myself from childhood have been a 'Good Friday Christian'. One Good Friday I was so weighed down with misery that my mother took me into the backyard to play ball. And I could not. That day I must mourn though only a child. Sometimes I have found it hard to preach at Easter after Holy Week kept so intensively, though as the Easter season proceeds and we read of the resurrection appearances, joy takes over. Easter is no fairy tale ending, it is 'an ultimate hope held in the very teeth of suffering and diminuation.'

The secret of living is not mighty resolutions of the will, but the way we see that determines the kind of beings that we are. If only we could see people properly we should be delivered at once from obsessive dislike or inordinate affection. Our faith in Christ is not solely or even primarily a matter of trying to understand arguments in favour of Christianity, or to reason ourselves into belief; it is learning to look to Jesus, what is often called contemplation – so that we see him in all things and all things in him. This lifts up our hearts and sets us free from that unholy and despairing worldliness which is earthbound.

There is a tragic element in Christianity. After two thousand years evil still stalks the earth. There is still violence and atrocity and some of it has been done under the sign of the Cross. We must not turn aside from this too easily in our longing to preach Christ's victory. It may have been the reason for his agony in the Garden. It makes the symbols of his Passion still relevant as we move into the third millennium. Jesus is alive. And this not because of the love he still inspires or even the remembrance he enjoined, vital as that is, but by the power of God. Christ still bears the marks of his Passion, if we would share his Easter we must share his Good Friday also.

The worst thing that can happen may somehow be transfigured and transcended in remembrance and in contemplation. This is what art does – the dire hopeless futilities of tragic events are given some purpose by what Sophocles and Shakespeare have done with them, just as slavery, that monstrous institution of unrelieved human blindness and brutality was transformed into spirituals, and the passion of Christ has become the liturgy of the Church. This is what Christian worship is about. It has been misrepresented, abused, made blasphemous by Christians, but it is the means, the art by which we come to terms with the worst that can happen.

Worship is not something which starts when the choir sings the introit or the Minister announces the first hymn. Worship began with the dawn of creation when the morning stars sang together. Worship is the eternal self offering of the Son to the Father and goes on without interruption, and all we can do as a church is to join ourselves to that. Our offering is always incomplete, our sacrifice imperfect, we 'do not presume to come'. But whenever we come we are always welcome. At any moment you can say, whatever your past failures or present wanderings, 'I will arise and go to my Father'.

We may receive revelations in our private prayers, and the contemplative life can be a stage on the way to holiness, to perfect love. But the whole truth is in the Lord's death and resurrection, his ascent into heaven and the gift of the Holy Spirit. Our personal experience is connected and transcended as we worship with the faithful on earth and the whole company of heaven. We exercise our priesthood as we pray for others, for by doing so we consecrate them to God. Prayer is an altar at which we officiate.

"He took Peter and James and John"

Why did Jesus require company? We are affirming one of the deepest paradoxes of Scripture and surely being true to the facts of what happened if we recognise that he took Peter and James and John because he wanted and needed them. True he had Moses and Elijah and "all the company of heaven" and above all his Father and his God. But all these were not enough. He took Peter and James and John. It is though he would say "I have Thy company but I must have theirs too". Their human nearness could be of some help to him, while the victory for which he fought and the kingdom he secured were not complete without them.

Christ was crucified not in a sacred building, but outside the city walls; in the world, the world of nature and of humankind, for it is the world he saves not just those with an interest in religion; it may be hardest of all to save them. And because the veil is rent, there is complete and free communication between earth and heaven, no distinction any more between sacred and secular. The sacred body of Jesus, not just his physical frame but his very self, which has passed through death is everywhere. There is no place where he is not, no place where we may not even here and now receive fullness of life.

It is not, I believe, without significance that the Revelation of St John which begins with the vision of the risen Christ, (so much more in the idiom of Epstein at Llandaff and Sutherland at Coventry, than of the Sunday School art of Jesus blessing the children,) ends with the vision of the city, the new Jerusalem. This is entirely logical. To see God is to enjoy the community life of a heaven and earth redeemed. That is the vision which inspires us through the dreary days of a world, which with all its loveliness, to which we should be ever sensitive, is often drab and dispiriting. And our acts of worship and exercise of prayer should, please God, bring us some moments like Bunyan's pilgrim glimpsing the Delectable Mountains.

Teachers today would think it excessive or inappropriate to lower their voices, as did James Hope Moulton, once Professor of New Testament and Comparative Religion, whenever he mentioned the name of Jesus. But the person of Christ as fulfilled in continuing history, should capture our imagination and our devotion. There is still a living power and a love which streams from his life and death and may sustain us in all our vicissitudes, in a world in some ways more bleak and sorrowful than his. He says to us as to Peter 'Do you love me?' Will you not reply from the circle of his friends?

> Lord it is my chief complaint
> That my love is weak and faint
> Yet I love thee and adore
> O for grace to love thee more.